94063244R00057

Made in the USA
Lexington, KY
22 July 2018